SAIF HUSSAINI

Effective Communication Skills: Speak with Confidence, Work Smarter, Achieve More

Mastering the Power of Speech in Work and Life – Your Guide to Being a Leader

Contents

V   Part V: Real-World Applications and Case Studies

Introduction

The Importance of Effective Communication

Embracing the Power of Words

In the tapestry of human interaction, every thread is a word, a gesture, a glance. And the most vibrant of these threads are those woven with the art of effective communication. As an author who has traversed the valleys and peaks of countless conversations, I've witnessed firsthand the transformative magic of well-chosen words and the silent, yet profound language of empathy.

The Definition: More Than Words

What, then, is effective communication? It is not merely the exchange of words, the idle chit-chat by the water cooler, nor the routine 'good mornings' exchanged with neighbors. It is an orchestra of verbal and non-verbal cues, each note playing its part in harmony. It's the art of understanding and being understood, where every gesture, every inflection, every silence speaks volumes.

The Canvas of Our Lives: Personal and Professional Worlds

In our personal lives, effective communication is the golden key that unlocks deeper connections. Imagine a world where every 'I understand', truly means it, where every 'I'm here for you', is more than a mere phrase. Picture a dinner table where stories are not just heard, but felt, where laughter is shared, not just echoed. This is the world effective communication creates – one rich in connection and understanding.

In the professional arena, effective communication is the lighthouse guiding ships through a fog of uncertainties. It's the difference between a team that works like a well-oiled machine and one that stumbles in misunderstanding. Remember the last time a leader's speech left you invigorated, ready to climb mountains? That's the power of effective communication at work.

The Silent Symphony: A Personal Anecdote

Let me share a moment from my own life – a silent symphony that still echoes in my heart. Years ago, during a critical business meeting, I realized that words were failing us. Amidst the heated discussion, I paused, took a deep breath, and simply listened. The room fell silent. In that silence, we found clarity. It wasn't a battle of words, but a ballet of understanding. That day, we didn't just reach an agreement; we built a bridge.

The Ripple Effect: Transforming the Future

Effective communication does more than resolve conflicts or build bonds; it has a ripple effect, transforming the future. It's the soft but steady rain that nurtures the fields of our relationships, allowing trust and respect to bloom. It's the wind that sails our professional ships towards horizons of unparalleled success.

As we stand on the threshold of countless interactions, let us remember the power we wield – the power to change a moment, a day, a life. Through mastering the art of effective communication, we don't just speak; we resonate. We don't just listen; we understand. We don't just exist together; we thrive together.

In these pages that follow, we will look into the heart of effective communication, not just to learn a skill, but to transform the very essence of our interactions. Let's embrace this adventure, not just as a learning experience, but as a beacon that lights up the path to a world where every word, every silence, every gesture, makes a difference.

Welcome to the art of effective communication. Welcome to a brighter, more connected world.

Why Effective Communication Matters in Personal and Professional Life

The Symphony of Human Connection

In the grand theater of life, effective communication is the music that binds the performers and the audience in an unseen, yet unbreakable bond. It is the heartbeat of human connection, pulsing in our personal and professional worlds, bringing us closer to those around us, and propelling us towards shared goals and dreams.

In Personal Relationships: Building Bridges, Not Walls

In the intimate dance of personal relationships, effective communication is the rhythm that keeps us in step with our loved ones. It's not just about talking, but about truly connecting. Imagine a world where families not only share a meal but also share their deepest fears and greatest joys, where friends understand without judgment, where love is expressed not only in words but in understanding and empathy.

I recall a time when a simple conversation with a dear friend turned into a profound moment of connection. We shared stories, not just as a form of expression, but as a way of offering pieces of ourselves. In that exchange, we didn't just speak; we wove a tapestry of trust and companionship that still envelops us to this day.

In the Professional Sphere: The Currency of Success

In the bustling marketplace of professional life, effective communication is the currency of success. It's the spark that ignites innovation, the glue that binds a team together, and the compass that guides leaders to inspire and motivate. Picture a workplace where every idea is heard and valued, where feedback is a ladder to excellence, where visions are shared, and goals are achieved in unison.

There was a moment in my career when a project teetered on the edge of failure. It was communication, clear, honest, and purposeful, that turned the tides. We didn't just exchange information; we shared a vision, and in that sharing, we found the pathway to success.

The Butterfly Effect: Small Words, Big Impact

Every word we utter, every listen we lend, sets off a butterfly effect, shaping our future. In personal ties, effective communication fosters understanding and deepens bonds, turning houses into homes and acquaintances into lifelong friends. In the professional world, it builds bridges of collaboration, turning individual efforts into collective triumphs.

The Invitation to Transform

As we turn into the pages ahead, we start on a transformative experience. Each chapter is an invitation to unlock the potential that effective communication holds – to build stronger relationships, to achieve professional excellence, to lead with conviction, and to connect with the world in ways you never imagined.

Let this book be your guide to mastering the art of effective communication. Together, we will uncover the secrets of words spoken, unspoken, and those yet to be said. Let's embrace the power of communication and witness its ability to transform our lives and the world around us.

Welcome to the world where effective communication opens doors to endless possibilities. Welcome to a brighter future, sculpted by the art of communication.

I

Part I: Foundations of Effective Communication

Chapter 1: Understanding Communication Basics

1.1 Elements of Communication: Sender, Message, Receiver, Feedback

In the realm of communication, four fundamental elements converge to create a tapestry of understanding: the sender, the message, the receiver, and the feedback. Each plays a crucial role, harmonizing to transform simple exchanges into meaningful dialogue.

The Sender: The Voice Initiating the Dialogue

The sender is the initiator, the one who starts the conversation. Their role transcends merely speaking or writing; it involves the thoughtful crafting of the message. The tone, the choice of words, even the timing, all shape how the message is conveyed and perceived.

The Message: The Heartbeat of Communication

At the core lies the message, the essence of what is being communicated. It's an amalgamation of thoughts, emotions, and intentions, woven into words. A clear, well-articulated message can bridge gaps, foster understanding, and inspire change.

The Receiver: The Interpreter of the Message

The receiver is the interpreter, bringing their own perceptions, experiences, and biases to the conversation. Their understanding can profoundly shape the communication's outcome, highlighting the importance of considering the receiver's perspective.

Feedback: The Reflection That Guides Improvement

Finally, feedback acts as a mirror, reflecting how the message was received and understood. It's a vital component, offering the sender insight into the effectiveness of their communication and providing an opportunity for adjustment and growth.

A Symphony of Understanding: A Personal Reflection

Reflecting on these elements brings to mind a pivotal moment in my professional life. I was presenting a complex proposal to a diverse group of stakeholders. The message was intricate, requiring careful explanation. As the sender, I had to ensure clarity and engagement. The words chosen, the pauses for emphasis, the responses to their nonverbal cues - all were critical in ensuring the message was not just delivered but also understood and appreciated.

The turning point was the feedback – a mix of affirming nods, inquisitive questions, and thoughtful critiques. This feedback was the guiding light, showing me which parts of the message resonated and where further clarification was needed. It transformed a mere presentation into a dynamic conversation, a two-way street of understanding and collaboration.

This experience underscored the delicate interplay of the sender, message, receiver, and feedback. It was a vivid reminder of how each element is crucial in crafting effective communication, whether in personal conversations, professional discussions, or impactful presentations.

1.2 Verbal, Non-Verbal, and Written Communication

In the realm of human interaction, communication emerges not just as an exchange of information, but as a rich tapestry woven from verbal, non-verbal, and written strands. Each form has its unique melody and rhythm, playing a vital role in how we connect and understand each other.

Verbal Communication: The Symphony of Spoken Words

Verbal communication is the music of our spoken words. It's the rhythm and tone of our voice, the emphasis we place on certain words, and the emotions that resonate through our speech. It's not merely the content of our words, but the way we articulate them that breathes life into our conversations.

Non-Verbal Communication: The Silent Dance of Understanding

Non-verbal communication is the silent dance that accompanies our words. It's the subtle gestures, the flickers of expression across our face, the stance of our body. This unspoken orchestra can often convey more meaning than words alone, painting a fuller picture of our intentions and feelings.

Written Communication: The Canvas of Our Thoughts

Written communication is the canvas where our words are painted in ink or pixels, leaving a lasting imprint. It's the craft of articulating thoughts, emotions, and information through the written word, be it through letters, emails, or texts. In our digital age, this form of communication is more crucial than ever, offering a means to convey complex ideas and emotions across time and space.

A Harmony of Forms: A Personal Reflection

Reflecting on these elements brings to mind a significant moment from my own experiences. I was tasked with addressing a diverse group, each individual coming from a unique background. The challenge was not just in what I had to say but in how it needed to be communicated.

The verbal aspect was crucial – choosing words that were inclusive, a tone that was engaging, and a pace that allowed for absorption. Yet, equally important were my non-verbal cues – the openness of my stance, the inclusivity of my gestures, and the sincerity in my eye contact.

Following the event, I penned a detailed written summary, ensuring that the essence of my message was captured in a form that could be revisited and reflected upon. This exercise was a powerful reminder of the intertwining nature of verbal, non-verbal, and written communication, each supporting and enhancing the other.

The Power of Three: Shaping Our Interactions

As we move forward, understanding these three forms of communication will empower us to convey our messages more effectively and forge deeper connections. The mastery of verbal, non-verbal, and written communication is not just about transferring information; it's about creating understanding, building relationships, and sharing our human experience. Let's embrace these forms of communication, using them to paint our interactions with the colors of clarity, empathy, and depth.

Chapter 2: Common Communication Barriers

2.1 Physical, Psychological, Language, and Cultural Barriers

In the symphony of communication, barriers can arise like unexpected notes, altering the melody and harmony we strive to create. Recognizing and understanding these barriers – physical, psychological, language, and cultural – is the first step in transforming them from obstacles into opportunities for deeper understanding and connection.

Physical Barriers: Beyond the Obvious Obstacles

Physical barriers are the tangible obstructions in our environment that hinder communication. They can range from a poorly designed meeting room that stifles conversation to the vast distances separating individuals in our increasingly global world. These barriers, while seemingly insurmountable, can often be overcome with thoughtful adjustments and technological advancements.

Psychological Barriers: The Invisible Walls

More elusive are the psychological barriers. These are the internal battles, the fears, prejudices, and biases that each of us carries. They are the filters through which we interpret the world, and they can significantly distort the true essence of our communication. Overcoming these requires introspection, empathy, and a commitment to personal growth.

Language Barriers: The Puzzle of Words

Language barriers go beyond just speaking different tongues. It's also the jargon, the professional lingo, the regional colloquialisms that can make our messages cryptic to others. To bridge these gaps, we must strive for clarity, simplicity, and understanding.

Cultural Barriers: The Tapestry of Diversity

Cultural barriers are perhaps the most intricate. Our cultural backgrounds shape our beliefs, behaviors, and ways of communicating. Misunderstandings can arise from differing cultural norms and values, but these barriers also present a rich opportunity for learning and growth.

A Story of Overcoming Barriers: My Own Encounter

Reflecting on these barriers, I am reminded of a significant episode in my professional life. I was leading a diverse team spread across multiple countries, each member bringing their unique cultural and linguistic background to the table. The challenge was not just the physical distance, but the multitude of psychological, language, and cultural barriers that

9

lay between us.

In one instance, a crucial project was faltering due to miscommunications and misunderstandings. It was a jarring wake-up call. I
realized that for us to succeed, we needed to turn these barriers into
bridges. We started with open conversations, acknowledging and
sharing our individual challenges. We adopted technologies that bridged
our physical distance, but more importantly, we made an effort to learn
and appreciate each other's cultural and linguistic nuances.

This experience taught me that the power to overcome communication
barriers lies not in erasing our differences, but in embracing and
understanding them. It was a lesson in the beauty of diversity and the
strength that comes from unity in variety.

Transforming Barriers into Bridges

As we explore these common communication barriers, let us view
them not as hindrances but as opportunities to forge stronger, more
empathetic, and more effective connections. Each barrier overcome is a
step towards a world where diversity is celebrated, and understanding
is deepened. Let's embrace this opportunity to turn our communication
barriers into bridges, leading to a richer, more connected world.

2.2 Overcoming Barriers

In the landscape of communication, barriers are not dead ends, but
rather stepping stones towards greater understanding and connection
Overcoming these barriers is an art in itself, requiring patience, creativ-
ity, and a deep sense of empathy.

Embracing Technology: Bridging Physical Distances

In an age where technology has leaped forward, physical distances shrink under its touch. Video conferencing, instant messaging, and collaborative online platforms have opened doors to seamless interaction, regardless of geographical divides. These tools are not just conduits of words; they are bridges that connect us, heart to heart, across miles.

Psychological Empathy: Understanding Beyond Words

To overcome psychological barriers, the key lies in empathy. It's about listening with an open heart, understanding that each person's perception is their reality. It involves breaking down our own walls of prejudice and embracing vulnerability. When we approach communication with empathy, we not only hear what is being said, but we also understand what is left unsaid.

Simplifying Language: The Clarity in Communication

Language barriers are surmounted by simplifying our speech and writing. It's about making our message as clear and jargon-free as possible. Using simple language does not dilute our message; rather, it amplifies its clarity, ensuring that what we wish to convey is not lost in translation.

Cultural Sensitivity: A Celebration of Diversity

Overcoming cultural barriers requires a celebration of diversity. It's about taking the time to learn about and respect other cultural norms and values. When we approach communication with a mindset of cultural sensitivity, we open ourselves up to a world of rich, diverse perspectives that can significantly enrich our own understanding and experiences.

A Personal Chronicle of Overcoming Barriers

Let me share a poignant episode that encapsulates the essence of overcoming these barriers. I was part of a project that brought together individuals from various cultural and linguistic backgrounds. The initial meetings were riddled with misunderstandings – a clear indication of the barriers we were up against.

We took a proactive approach. We started with cultural exchange sessions, where each team member shared insights into their cultural norms and communication styles. We embraced technology to ensure no one was left out due to physical distance. We adopted a rule of simplicity in language to make sure everyone was on the same page. But most importantly, we fostered an environment of empathy and understanding.

The transformation was remarkable. Not only did the project succeed, but it also left us with a deeper understanding and appreciation of each other's backgrounds. This experience was a testament to the fact that when barriers are viewed not as obstacles but as opportunities for growth, the potential for success is limitless.

Building Bridges of Understanding

As we move through this chapter, let us remember that the power to overcome communication barriers lies within us. It's about changing our perspective, adopting new tools, and opening our

hearts to empathy and understanding. With each step we take to bridge these divides, we not only enhance our communication skills but also enrich our lives with deeper connections and broader perspectives.

Let this chapter serve as a guide and an inspiration to transform the way we communicate, turning barriers into gateways of mutual understanding and respect. Let's commit to building bridges, not just in our words, but through our actions and intentions, creating a world where every voice is heard and every message is valued.

II

Part II: Key Communication Skills

Chapter 3: Listening Skills

3.1 Active Listening Techniques

In the symphony of communication, listening is not just a passive act; it is an active engagement, a deliberate effort to not just hear, but to understand, to empathize, and to connect. Active listening is the cornerstone of effective communication, a skill that transforms conversations and deepens relationships.

The Art of Attentive Listening

Active listening starts with full attention. It's the act of focusing entirely on the speaker, shutting out the noise of distractions and preconceptions. This attentiveness signals to the speaker that their words are valuable, that their thoughts and feelings matter.

Reflective Listening: Echoing Understanding

Reflective listening is an integral part of active listening. It involves paraphrasing or summarizing what the speaker has said, not merely to respond but to demonstrate understanding. This reflection shows that we are not just hearing their words, but also processing and valuing them.

Asking Probing Questions

Active listening is further enriched by asking questions - not intrusive, but probing questions that encourage deeper exploration of the speaker's thoughts and feelings. This technique helps in peeling back layers, revealing the core of the speaker's message.

Non-Verbal Cues: Silent Signals of Engagement

Non-verbal cues, such as nodding, maintaining eye contact, and appropriate facial expressions, reinforce active listening. They are the unspoken words that say, "I am with you, I am listening."

A Personal Tale of Active Listening

Let me share a personal experience that underscores the power of active listening. During a critical team meeting, a member was struggling to articulate a complex idea. The room was growing restless, but I sensed an underlying brilliance in his stammering words.

I turned my full attention to him, nodding and maintaining eye contact. I paraphrased his points for clarity and asked open-ended questions to help him express his thoughts more clearly. As the conversation unfolded, his confidence grew, his words found their rhythm, and his idea blossomed into a strategy that later proved to be a turning point for our project.

This experience was a vivid reminder of the transformative power of active listening. It wasn't just about giving him space to speak; it was about creating an environment where he felt heard and understood. That day, active listening did not just facilitate effective communication; it fostered trust, respect, and a sense of belonging within the team.

Cultivating a Culture of Listening

Active listening is not just a skill; it's a commitment to building a culture of mutual respect and understanding. It's about setting aside our own agendas and immersing ourselves in the world of the speaker. When we listen actively, we open doors to new perspectives, deeper insights, and stronger connections.

In the following sections, we will explore practical techniques and exercises to hone your active listening skills. This journey is about transforming not just how you listen, but how you connect, empathize, and engage with those around you. Let's embrace the art of active listening, turning every conversation into an opportunity for growth and connection.

3.2 Understanding and Empathy in Listening

In the vast ocean of communication, understanding and empathy are the lighthouses that guide us to truly connect with others. Listening with understanding and empathy is about immersing ourselves in the speaker's world, feeling their emotions, and seeing through their eyes. This level of listening goes beyond the surface, reaching the depths of human connection.

The Essence of Empathetic Listening

Empathetic listening is the heart of true understanding. It's about connecting with the emotions behind the words. This form of listening is not just about comprehending the spoken language but about tuning into the emotional frequencies of the speaker.

The Power of Validation

Validating the speaker's feelings and perspectives is a crucial aspect of empathetic listening. It's a way of acknowledging their emotions and experiences as real and significant. This validation is not about agreement but about respect and acknowledgment of their feelings.

Pausing and Reflecting

In empathetic listening, pausing before responding is vital. It allows us to fully absorb the speaker's message and emotions. Reflecting on what's been said before jumping into a response shows that we value their words and are considering them thoughtfully.

A Personal Encounter with Empathy

I recall a profound moment where empathetic listening transformed a challenging situation. A colleague was facing a personal crisis, and her distress was affecting her work. During a conversation, instead of offering solutions or advice, I chose to simply listen – to understand, to feel her pain, and to acknowledge her struggle.

This approach opened up a space where she felt seen and heard. My responses were not about fixing her problem but about validating her feelings. This empathy created a bond of trust and understanding, which later translated into a stronger, more supportive work relationship.

It was a powerful reminder that sometimes, the best way to help is just to listen with empathy and understanding. In doing so, we provide a safe haven for others to express themselves and feel supported.

Fostering a Future of Empathetic Connections

As we dive deeper into understanding and empathy in listening, let's aim to cultivate these skills not just as communicators but as human beings. Empathetic listening has the power to transform relationships, resolve conflicts, and build a world where everyone feels heard and valued. Let's commit to listening not just with our ears, but with our hearts, fostering a future where empathy and understanding are at the forefront of every conversation.

Chapter 4: Verbal Communication

4.1 Articulation and Clarity

In the realm of verbal communication, articulation and clarity are the twin pillars that uphold the structure of effective expression. They transform mere words into powerful tools of connection and understanding. Mastering these skills is not just about being heard; it's about being understood, about bridging the gap between thought and expression.

The Art of Articulation

Articulation is the precision and clarity in the way we form words. It's the fine art of speaking so that each word is distinct and contributes to the overall coherence of the message. Articulate speech is a melody that flows smoothly, captivating the listener with its clarity and ease.

Clarity: The Clear Stream of Thought

Clarity in communication is about conveying your thoughts in a straightforward and unambiguous manner. It's the skill of organizing your thoughts and presenting them in a way that leaves little room for misunderstanding. Clear communication is like a stream flowing unhindered, delivering its contents directly and effectively.

The Interplay of Thought and Speech

The harmony between thought and speech is crucial in achieving articulation and clarity. It's about aligning your words with your thoughts, ensuring that your speech is a true and clear reflection of your mind.

A Personal Reflection on Clarity

Reflecting on the importance of articulation and clarity brings to mind a crucial presentation early in my career. I was tasked with explaining a complex concept to a diverse audience. The challenge was not just in the complexity of the topic, but in ensuring that each member of the audience would grasp the essence of what I was conveying.

I meticulously planned each sentence, choosing my words for maximum clarity and impact. During the presentation, I focused on articulating each word, ensuring I was not only heard but understood. The result was a successful communication of ideas, and the feedback I received highlighted the effectiveness of clear and articulate speech.

This experience was a powerful reminder of the transformative power of articulation and clarity in verbal communication. It reinforced the idea that the way we express our thoughts can significantly impact the understanding and engagement of our audience.

The Path to Articulate and Clear Communication

As we explore the nuances of articulation and clarity, remember that these skills are not just tools for effective communication; they are bridges that connect minds and hearts. Let's embrace the art of clear and articulate speech, transforming our words into keys that unlock understanding and connection. In doing so, we not only enhance our ability to express ourselves but also contribute to a world where every voice is not just heard, but understood.

4.2 Tone, Pace, and Volume

In the orchestra of verbal communication, tone, pace, and volume are like the unique instruments that give character to our speech. They add color, emotion, and intensity to our words, shaping how our message is perceived and received. Mastering these aspects of speech is akin to a conductor skillfully guiding the orchestra to create a harmonious symphony.

The Resonance of Tone

Tone is the emotional undercurrent of our words, the subtle indicator of our true feelings. It's the warmth in a friendly greeting, the sternness in a warning, the compassion in words of comfort. Our tone has the power to build trust, to soothe, to energize, or even to alienate.

The Rhythm of Pace

Pace is the rhythm of our speech. A measured, deliberate pace can convey confidence and clarity, while a rapid pace can express excitement or urgency. However, speaking too fast can overwhelm the listener, just as speaking too slowly can diminish their interest.

The Impact of Volume

Volume, the loudness or softness of our voice, is a tool for emphasizing points and expressing intensity. A raised voice can command attention or express strong emotion, while a whisper can draw listeners in, creating intimacy or suspense.

A Symphony of Expression: My Personal Experience

I once faced a situation where understanding the interplay of tone, pace, and volume was crucial. I was leading a team through a difficult phase in a project. Morale was low, and there was palpable tension in the air.

During a crucial team meeting, I was mindful of how I used my voice. I started with a calm, steady tone, setting a foundation of stability and confidence. My pace was deliberate, allowing my words to sink in and giving space for the team to absorb the message. I varied my volume, speaking softly to draw them into the narrative of our shared goal, then increasing volume to emphasize our collective strength and resilience.

This mindful orchestration of tone, pace, and volume turned the meeting into a turning point. It reignited the team's passion and refocused our efforts. The change in the atmosphere was palpable – from one of uncertainty to one of unified determination. This experience underscored the profound impact our vocal expression can have on the spirit and dynamics of a group.

The Art of Vocal Expression

As we explore the nuances of tone, pace, and volume, remember that these are not just aspects of speech; they are powerful tools for emotional connection and persuasion. They have the capacity to transform our interactions, to captivate, to motivate, and to inspire.

Let us embrace the art of vocal expression, using tone, pace, and volume not just to speak, but to truly communicate. Let's use our voices to paint vivid pictures, to touch hearts, and to move minds. By mastering these elements, we open up a world of possibilities in how we connect with others, bringing our words to life in ways that resonate deeply and leave a lasting impact.

Chapter 5: Non-Verbal Communication

5.1 Body Language

In the silent music of communication, body language is a powerful melody. It speaks without words, conveying emotions and intentions through the movements and postures of our body. Mastering body language is akin to learning a subtle yet profound dance, where every gesture contributes to the story we tell.

The Dance of Posture

Posture is the backbone of body language. A straight, open posture can convey confidence and openness, while a slouched or closed posture might suggest discomfort or disinterest. The way we stand, sit, or move not only communicates our feelings to others but also influences our own mental state.

The Grace of Gestures

Gestures, be they the expressive movement of hands or the subtle tilting of the head, are the accents in the language of the body. They can emphasize a point, express enthusiasm, or show empathy. Gestures are like brushstrokes in a painting, adding depth and emotion to the picture we are painting with our words.

The Symphony of Synchronization

Synchronizing our body language with our words adds a layer of authenticity to our communication. When our gestures and posture align with our verbal message, it creates a harmony that resonates with authenticity and credibility.

A Personal Symphony of Body Language

I recall a significant moment in my career when body language played a pivotal role. I was negotiating a crucial deal, and the stakes were high. As the discussion progressed, I noticed that my counterpart's posture had shifted from a defensive, arms-crossed position to a more open, forward-leaning stance. Mirroring his posture, I leaned in slightly, gesturing openly as I spoke.

This subtle dance of body language created a bridge of trust and understanding. It was as if our bodies were having a conversation parallel to our words, each gesture and posture shift echoing our willingness to find common ground. This non-verbal harmony paved the way for a successful conclusion to our negotiation, a testament to the unspoken power of body language.

The Unspoken Art of Communication

As we explore the nuances of body language, let us remember that our bodies can speak volumes even in silence. The way we carry ourselves the gestures we use, and the postures we adopt are integral parts of our communication repertoire.

Let's embrace the art of body language, using it to enhance our verbal communication and to express what words alone cannot convey. By becoming fluent in this unspoken language, we open up new dimensions in our interactions, creating deeper connections and more meaningful experiences. In mastering body language, we don't just communicate; we connect on a level that transcends words, in the beautiful silence of understanding.

5.2 Eye Contact, Facial Expressions, and Gestures

The subtle art of non-verbal communication extends beyond body language to the realms of eye contact, facial expressions, and gestures. These elements are the fine details in the canvas of communication, offering depth and emotion to the picture painted by our words.

The Window of the Soul: Eye Contact

Eye contact is the bridge that connects two minds, a powerful tool for engagement and understanding. It conveys attention, interest, and respect. Maintaining appropriate eye contact signifies that we are fully present, creating a sense of connection and trust between the speaker and the listener. However, it's also a delicate balance – too little, and we may seem disinterested; too much, and we risk intimidation.

The Silent Conversations: Facial Expressions

Facial expressions are the unspoken words of our emotions. A smile, a frown, a raised eyebrow – these subtle shifts can convey a spectrum of feelings and reactions. They are the nuances that give color to our words, the silent conversations that happen even before a word is spoken.

The Language of Gestures

Gestures are the punctuation marks of our non-verbal communication, accentuating and emphasizing our verbal messages. A nod can affirm, a wave can welcome, and a hand gesture can highlight a crucial point. Gestures are like the brushstrokes in a painting, each one adding a layer of meaning and emotion to our communication.

A Personal Tale of Non-Verbal Mastery

I remember a defining moment where these elements of non-verbal communication played a crucial role. I was facilitating a workshop with a diverse group, each participant bringing their unique perspectives and communication styles.

One participant, particularly reserved, rarely spoke but communicated volumes through her non-verbal cues. Initially, her minimal eye contact and closed-off facial expressions suggested disengagement. However, as I consciously used open gestures and maintained gentle, inclusive eye contact, I noticed a gradual shift. Her facial expressions softened, and her gestures became more expressive, mirroring the warmth and openness of the environment we were cultivating.

This experience was a profound reminder of the power of eye contact, facial expressions, and gestures in creating an atmosphere of inclusivity and understanding. It was a lesson in how these subtle cues can invite participation and encourage expression in ways that words alone may not achieve.

CHAPTER 5: NON-VERBAL COMMUNICATION

The Symphony of Silent Understanding

As we dig into the intricacies of eye contact, facial expressions, and gestures, let us recognize their immense power in enriching our communication. These non-verbal elements can build bridges of understanding, break down walls of misunderstanding, and deepen our connections with those around us.

Let's harness the power of these silent communicators, using them to complement and enhance our verbal interactions. In doing so, we open up a world of deeper understanding and more meaningful connections, where every glance, every smile, and every gesture plays its part in the beautiful symphony of human communication.

Chapter 6: Written Communication

6.1 Writing Clear and Concise Emails, Reports, and Texts

In the digital age, the written word is a powerful tool, a bridge connecting ideas across the expanse of time and space. Writing clear and concise emails, reports, and texts is an art form, one that combines the elegance of simplicity with the precision of clarity. Mastering this art is essential in a world where written communication often forms the first and lasting impression.

The Essence of Clarity and Conciseness

Clarity in writing is like a beacon in the fog, guiding the reader to the heart of your message without the haze of ambiguity. Conciseness, on the other hand, is the art of being succinct, conveying your message without unnecessary adornment. Together, they make your writing not just effective but impactful.

Structuring for Impact

Effective structuring is the skeleton of good writing. It involves organizing your thoughts in a logical flow, making your message easy to follow and understand. A well-structured email or report guides the reader through your points seamlessly, like a well-plotted path through a garden, allowing them to appreciate every turn and every view.

The Power of the Right Words

Choosing the right words is akin to selecting the right colors for a painting. Each word should add value and meaning, painting a clear picture of your intent and message. The right words can turn a simple email into a compelling read, a report into a persuasive document.

A Personal Chronicle in Writing

I recall a pivotal moment in my career when the power of clear and concise writing became evident. I was tasked with drafting a crucial proposal under a tight deadline. The challenge was not just the complexity of the subject but the need to make it accessible and engaging for a diverse audience.

I focused on structuring my thoughts clearly, breaking down complex ideas into digestible parts. I chose my words carefully, ensuring they conveyed the essence of the proposal without unnecessary jargon. The final document was a concise, clear, and persuasive piece that not only won us the project but also earned praise for its clarity and ease of understanding.

This experience was a testament to the power of clear and concise writing in opening doors and creating opportunities. It underscored the importance of crafting written communications that are not just read but understood and remembered.

The Art of Writing in the Digital Age

As we explore the nuances of writing clear and concise emails, reports, and texts, let us embrace the opportunity to refine our skills. Let's commit to writing not just to convey information, but to connect, persuade, and inspire. In mastering the art of written communication, we open ourselves to new possibilities and opportunities, making every word we write a step towards a future of clearer understanding and stronger connections.

6.2 Online Communication Etiquette

In the virtual realms where our words travel digitally, etiquette in online communication becomes the compass that guides our interactions. It's about more than just manners; it's about creating an environment of respect, clarity, and professionalism. In a world where emails and texts can be sent in a heartbeat, understanding the etiquette of online communication is crucial in maintaining and enhancing our personal and professional relationships.

The Art of Professionalism and Courtesy

Online communication, whether through emails or social media, calls for a balance of professionalism and courtesy. It's about respecting the invisible boundaries of digital space, acknowledging that behind every screen is a human with emotions and expectations.

Timeliness: The Essence of Respect

Responding in a timely manner is a cornerstone of online etiquette. It conveys respect and acknowledges the importance of the sender's message. A prompt response, even if it's an acknowledgment of receipt with a promise to follow up, can build trust and show your commitment to the communication.

Clarity and Tone: The Digital Voice

In the absence of face-to-face interaction, our words and their tone carry our message. Being clear and maintaining a respectful, friendly tone can prevent misunderstandings. It's about infusing our digital voice with warmth, making the recipient feel valued and heard.

A Story of Digital Misunderstanding and Learning

I recall an instance where the importance of online communication etiquette became strikingly clear to me. I had sent a hastily written email under stress, not realizing that my curt tone and brevity could be misconstrued. The recipient, a valued colleague, interpreted my message as dismissive and terse, leading to unnecessary tension.

This incident was a wake-up call about the power of words and tone in digital communication. I learned the importance of taking a moment to review my messages, ensuring they conveyed not just the information but also respect and consideration for the recipient.

The Future of Digital Interaction

As we move forward into an increasingly digital world, let's embrace the principles of online communication etiquette as essential tools for building and maintaining relationships. Let's use our digital interactions to spread positivity, understanding, and respect. By mastering online etiquette, we not only become better communicators but also contribute to a digital culture that is empathetic, respectful, and nurturing.

In mastering the art of online communication etiquette, we open ourselves to a world where every email, every text, and every digital interaction becomes an opportunity to build bridges, foster understanding, and create meaningful connections. Let's write not just with our keyboards, but with our hearts, transforming every digital interaction into a step towards a more connected and respectful world.

III

Part III: Advanced Communication Strategies

III

Part III: Advanced Communication
Strategies

Chapter 7: Emotional Intelligence in Communication

7.1 Recognizing and Managing Emotions

In the intricate dance of communication, emotional intelligence is the rhythm that harmonizes our words with our heartbeats. Recognizing and managing emotions in ourselves and others is not just a skill; it's an art form that transforms interactions into meaningful connections.

The Mirror of Self-Awareness

Self-awareness is the first step in mastering emotional intelligence. It's about holding a mirror to our emotions, understanding their origins, and recognizing their impact on our thoughts and communications. By being aware of our emotional state, we can manage our responses and communicate more effectively.

The Power of Self-Regulation

Once we recognize our emotions, the next step is self-regulation. This is the ability to control or redirect disruptive emotions and adapt to changing circumstances. It's about not letting a bad mood cloud our judgment or a burst of anger taint our words.

Emotional Agility in Communication

Emotional agility is navigating through our emotional landscape with grace and understanding. It's about being flexible with our emotions, understanding that they are transient and that our response to them shapes our communication.

A Personal Encounter with Emotional Intelligence

I recall a crucial meeting where emotional intelligence played a definitive role. A heated discussion had erupted, with strong opinions and rising tempers threatening to derail the meeting's purpose. Recognizing the emotional charge in the room, I took a moment to compose myself, breathing in calmness and exhaling the building frustration.

I then addressed the room, acknowledging the passion and emotions present. By first managing my own emotions, I was able to bring a level of calmness to the conversation. This shift in approach allowed everyone to take a step back, reassess their emotional state, and re-engage in a more constructive and respectful manner.

This experience was a profound reminder of the power of emotional intelligence in communication. It was a testament to how recognizing and managing our emotions can turn potentially destructive interactions into opportunities for collaborative problem-solving and deeper understanding.

The Path to Emotional Mastery in Communication

As we journey through the nuances of emotional intelligence, let's embrace the role of emotions in our communications. Let's strive to understand and regulate our emotions, not just for the sake of effective communication, but for building deeper, more empathetic connections with those around us.

In mastering the art of emotional intelligence, we unlock the potential to not just communicate, but to connect on a deeper, more meaningful level. It's a journey that not only enhances our communication skills but also enriches our relationships and personal growth. Let's embark on this path with an open heart and a willing mind, ready to transform our interactions into a tapestry woven with the threads of understanding, empathy, and emotional wisdom.

7.2 Communicating with Empathy

Empathy in communication is like a bridge built over a river of emotions, connecting two souls in the realm of understanding and compassion. It's about seeing the world through another's eyes, feeling what they feel, and communicating in a way that reflects this deep understanding.

The Essence of Empathetic Communication

Empathetic communication is about more than just understanding someone else's feelings. It's about sharing those feelings, acknowledging them, and responding in a way that validates their experience. It's a powerful tool that can transform relationships, resolve conflicts, and create a profound connection.

Active Listening: The Gateway to Empathy

Active listening is the first step towards empathetic communication. It involves fully concentrating on the speaker, understanding their message, and responding thoughtfully. It's about listening not just with ears but with the heart.

Responding with Sensitivity

Responding with sensitivity in empathetic communication involves acknowledging the other person's perspective and emotions. It's about choosing words that show understanding and compassion, and avoiding judgment or dismissal of their feelings.

A Personal Experience with Empathy

I recall a deeply moving experience where empathetic communication made a significant impact. A colleague was going through a tough time, and her performance at work was suffering. Instead of a standard managerial conversation about productivity, I chose to speak with her from a place of empathy.

We sat down, and I simply asked her how she was doing, genuinely wanting to understand her situation. As she opened up about her struggles, I listened intently, acknowledging her feelings and offering words of support. This approach not only helped in easing her burden but also strengthened our relationship and trust.

This encounter was a vivid reminder of the power of empathy in communication. It taught me that sometimes, the best way to solve a problem is not through direct advice or solutions, but through understanding and empathy.

Fostering Empathetic Connections

As we explore empathetic communication, let's remember its trans-formative power. By communicating with empathy, we're not just exchanging information; we're building connections, healing wounds, and bringing light into each other's lives.

Let's embrace the power of empathetic communication, using it to touch hearts, open minds, and build a world where everyone feels understood and valued. In doing so, we not only become better communicators but also contribute to a more compassionate, empathetic world.

Chapter 8: Conflict Resolution and Negotiation

8.1 Techniques for Resolving Disputes

In the tapestry of human interaction, conflicts are inevitable. They are the knots in the fabric that, when untangled skillfully, can strengthen the weave. Mastering the techniques for resolving disputes is not just about finding solutions; it's about transforming conflicts into opportunities for growth and understanding.

Understanding the Root of Conflict

The first step in resolving disputes is understanding their root cause. Conflicts often stem from unmet needs, misunderstood intentions, or clashing values. Unraveling these underlying issues is like following a thread back to where the knot began.

The Art of Active Listening

Active listening plays a crucial role in dispute resolution. It involves listening not just for the words being spoken but for the emotions and unspoken needs behind them. It's about creating a space where each party feels heard and validated.

Finding Common Ground

Finding common ground is the bridge that connects opposing sides in a conflict. It involves identifying shared values, goals, or interests that can serve as a foundation for building a solution. This shared ground becomes the platform upon which resolutions can be built.

A Personal Story of Resolving Conflict

I remember a challenging situation where these techniques came to life. Two team members were at loggerheads over a project's direction, each firmly entrenched in their viewpoint. The tension was palpable, affecting the entire team's morale.

I facilitated a meeting where each party had the opportunity to express their concerns without interruption. Through active listening, we uncovered that their conflict stemmed from a deep-seated fear of failure, a concern they both shared. Recognizing this common ground shifted the conversation from confrontation to collaboration.

We then worked together to find a solution that addressed both their concerns, turning a heated conflict into a constructive discussion. This experience was a powerful testament to the effectiveness of understanding, active listening, and finding common ground in resolving disputes.

The Path to Harmonious Resolutions

As we look into the techniques for resolving disputes, let's remember that each conflict presents an opportunity to strengthen relationships and build understanding. By approaching conflicts with empathy, active listening, and a focus on common ground, we can transform them into catalysts for positive change.

Let's embrace these techniques not just as tools for resolving disputes but as stepping stones to a future where conflicts are seen as opportunities for growth, understanding, and deeper connections. In mastering the art of conflict resolution, we open the door to more harmonious, collaborative, and fulfilling relationships.

8.2 Negotiation Tactics for Win-Win Outcomes

Negotiation is not just an exchange of demands; it's a ballet of balance a dance where each step is about finding harmony and mutual benefit Crafting win-win outcomes in negotiations is about seeing the bigger picture, where success is measured not just by what we gain, but by the relationships we build and nurture.

Understanding the Other Party's Perspective

The cornerstone of successful negotiation is understanding the other party's perspective. It's about stepping into their shoes, seeing the world through their eyes, and recognizing their needs and concerns This understanding lays the groundwork for a solution that respects and addresses the interests of all parties.

The Power of Empathy in Negotiation

Empathy in negotiation goes beyond understanding the other side's perspective; it's about genuinely caring for it. When we negotiate with empathy, we create a connection that transcends the transaction, building trust and opening doors to solutions that benefit everyone involved.

Creative Problem-Solving

Win-win negotiation is an exercise in creative problem-solving. It involves thinking outside the box, exploring options that might not be immediately apparent, and finding innovative ways to satisfy the needs of all parties.

A Personal Tale of Win-Win Negotiation

I recall a negotiation that was teetering on the brink of collapse. The stakes were high, and both sides were entrenched in their positions. I took a step back and focused on understanding the underlying needs of the other party, which were not just financial but also involved long-term partnership opportunities.

With this new understanding, I proposed a solution that not only met our immediate financial constraints but also offered a framework for future collaboration. This approach shifted the conversation from a tug-of-war over resources to a collaborative effort towards a shared vision.

The negotiation concluded not only with a successful deal but with the foundation for a strong, ongoing partnership. This experience was a testament to the power of empathy, understanding, and creative problem-solving in crafting win-win outcomes.

The Art of Harmonious Negotiation

As we explore negotiation tactics for win-win outcomes, let's remember that the most successful negotiations are those where all parties leave the table feeling heard, understood, and satisfied. Let's approach negotiation not as a battle to be won, but as an opportunity to build, to create, and to forge lasting relationships.

In mastering these tactics, we don't just achieve our goals; we create a ripple effect of positivity and collaboration, paving the way for a future where negotiation is synonymous with mutual respect, understanding, and shared success. Let's negotiate not just with our minds, but with our hearts, transforming every negotiation into a step towards a more understanding and collaborative world.

Chapter 9: Persuasion and Influence

9.1 Ethical Persuasion Techniques

In the grand theater of communication, persuasion is a subtle and powerful art. When wielded ethically, it's not about manipulation or coercion; it's about inspiring, motivating, and creating a vision that others feel compelled to share. Ethical persuasion is the golden thread that weaves together the fabric of influence and trust.

The Foundation of Ethical Persuasion

Ethical persuasion starts with the core principles of honesty and integrity. It's about presenting ideas and arguments that are not only compelling but also truthful and fair. This foundation ensures that the act of persuading others is grounded in respect and responsibility.

Understanding and Relating to the Audience

To persuade effectively, one must first understand and relate to the audience. It involves listening to their needs, understanding their viewpoints, and connecting your message to their values and beliefs. It's about crafting a narrative that resonates with them on a personal level.

The Power of Storytelling

Storytelling is a potent tool in ethical persuasion. A well-told story can captivate the imagination, stir emotions, and create a lasting impact. It's about weaving facts with narratives that engage the audience, making your message not just heard but felt.

A Personal Experience with Ethical Persuasion

I recall a significant moment where ethical persuasion played a crucial role. I was leading an initiative that required buy-in from multiple stakeholders, each with their own reservations and concerns. Instead of resorting to pressure tactics, I chose to engage them through storytelling, weaving in factual information with narratives that highlighted the mutual benefits and positive impact of the initiative.

I focused on understanding their perspectives and tailored my communication to address their specific concerns and aspirations. This approach not only garnered their support but also strengthened our relationships based on mutual respect and trust.

This experience underscored the effectiveness of ethical persuasion. It taught me that the most powerful persuasion comes from a place of empathy, understanding, and respect for the audience's needs and values.

The Art of Positive Influence

As we explore the techniques of ethical persuasion, let's embrace the responsibility that comes with this power. Let's use persuasion to inspire positive change, to kindle imagination, and to build a future where ideas are shared and embraced on the foundation of trust and respect.

In mastering ethical persuasion, we don't just influence decisions; we inspire action, we nurture trust, and we become architects of a future shaped by shared visions and collective aspirations. Let's weave our words with integrity and empathy, turning every act of persuasion into a step towards a more understanding, collaborative, and inspired world.

9.2 Building Trust and Credibility

In the orchestra of persuasion and influence, trust and credibility are the harmonious melodies that resonate with the soul of your audience. They are not just attributes to be displayed but virtues to be cultivated. Building trust and credibility is about creating a legacy of integrity, a pathway where others feel inspired and confident to follow.

The Pillars of Trust

Trust is the cornerstone of all meaningful relationships. It's built over time, through consistent actions, truthfulness, and reliability. In the context of persuasion, trust is about being genuine in your intentions and transparent in your communications.

Credibility: The Badge of Authenticity

Credibility is earned by demonstrating expertise and knowledge, but it's also about admitting when you don't have all the answers. It's a balance of confidence and humility, of expertise and continuous learning. Credibility is the badge that shows your audience that you are not just knowledgeable but also authentic.

Consistency: The Key to Reliability

Consistency in your words and actions reinforces trust and credibility. It's about aligning your actions with your values and promises. Consistency shows your audience that you are reliable, predictable, and worthy of their trust and respect.

A Personal Story of Trust Building

I recall a project where building trust and credibility was pivotal. I was leading a team through uncharted waters, and the uncertainty was high. I realized early on that to persuade my team to embrace this challenge, I needed to build trust and establish my credibility.

I did this by being open about the risks and potential rewards. I shared my own experiences and vulnerabilities, making it clear that while I had a vision, I valued their input and expertise. I was consistent in my communications and actions, always aligning them with the values and goals we had set as a team.

This approach not only won their trust but also fostered a sense of shared ownership over the project.

It transformed our journey from one of apprehension to one of collaborative adventure. The project turned out to be a remarkable success, not just in its outcomes, but in the trust and credibility it built within the team. This experience was a powerful testament to the fact that when trust and credibility are the foundation, even the loftiest goals become attainable.

The Art of Fostering Belief and Confidence

As we explore the art of building trust and credibility, let's remember that these are not just strategies but commitments to our personal and professional integrity. They are about walking the talk, being consistent in our actions, and being honest in our communications.

Let's embrace these principles not just to enhance our ability to persuade and influence, but to forge deeper connections, foster lasting relationships, and inspire others to believe in our vision. In cultivating trust and credibility, we don't just lead; we empower, creating a legacy of influence that is based on mutual respect and shared values.

In mastering the art of building trust and credibility, we open the door to a world where our words and actions align, where our influence is a reflection of our integrity, and where our leadership inspires confidence and belief. Let's commit to this path with a heart full of sincerity and a vision brimming with possibilities, turning every interaction into a stepping stone towards a future of trusted and credible influence.

IV

Part IV: Communication in Specific Contexts

Chapter 10: Professional Communication

10.1 In the Workplace

In the vibrant tapestry of professional life, communication is the thread that binds ideas, individuals, and intentions. Effective communication in the workplace is not just about exchanging information; it's about building a culture of understanding, respect, and collaboration. It's a dance of words and emotions, where every step, every gesture, contributes to the harmony of the workplace.

The Symphony of Clear Communication

Clarity in workplace communication is like the clear notes of a bell, resonating with precision and understanding. It involves conveying your ideas and thoughts in a straightforward manner, free from ambiguity. Clear communication reduces misunderstandings and paves the way for efficient and effective collaboration.

The Rhythm of Active Listening

Active listening in a professional setting is about tuning in with full attention, acknowledging, and understanding the viewpoints of others. It's about engaging with their ideas, providing feedback, and showing that their contributions are valued. This form of listening fosters a culture of mutual respect and openness.

The Harmony of Non-Verbal Cues

Non-verbal communication in the workplace, such as body language, eye contact, and facial expressions, plays a crucial role in reinforcing or contradicting our words. Aligning our non-verbal cues with our verbal messages enhances our ability to communicate effectively and authentically.

A Personal Story of Transformational Communication

I recall leading a team that was struggling with internal conflicts and miscommunications. The challenge was not just in what was being communicated but how it was being conveyed. I organized a series of workshops focusing on clear communication, active listening, and understanding non-verbal cues.

One particular session involved role-playing exercises, encouraging team members to express and interpret both verbal and non-verbal messages. This exercise opened our eyes to the nuances of our communication styles and how they affected others. The transformation in the team's dynamics was profound. Communication became more thoughtful, collaborative, and effective, leading to improved morale and productivity.

The Art of Effective Workplace Communication

As we dive into the art of professional communication in the workplace, let's be mindful of the power our words and actions hold. Let's commit to fostering an environment where clear communication, active listening, and understanding non-verbal cues are the norm, not the exception.

In mastering these skills, we not only enhance our professional interactions but also contribute to creating a workplace that thrives on mutual respect, understanding, and shared goals. Let's use our communication skills to build bridges, forge alliances, and create a workplace atmosphere where every voice is heard, and every message is valued.

10.2 Networking and Professional Relationships

In the constellation of professional life, networking and cultivating professional relationships are like navigating through a galaxy of opportunities and connections. These interactions are not just about exchanging business cards or LinkedIn connections; they are about building a tapestry of relationships that are enriched with trust, mutual respect, and genuine interest.

The Art of Authentic Networking

Authentic networking is about connecting on a level that transcends professional gain. It's about showing genuine interest in the person behind the title or the business. This approach transforms networking from a transactional experience to a relational journey.

Building Long-Term Relationships

The key to successful networking is the focus on building long-term relationships. It's about planting seeds of connection that can grow into partnerships, collaborations, or mentorships over time. It's not about 'what can you do for me,' but 'how can we support each other.'

The Dance of Reciprocity

Reciprocity is the rhythm that sustains professional relationships. It involves an exchange of value, be it in the form of knowledge, resources, or support. Reciprocity is not about keeping score but about creating a balance of give and take that benefits all parties involved.

A Personal Tale of Networking Transformation

I recall attending a networking event early in my career, feeling like a small fish in a big pond. Initially, I approached it with a transactional mindset, trying to make connections that would directly benefit my career. However, as the evening progressed, I shifted my approach, engaging in conversations with a genuine interest in learning about the other person's experiences and challenges.

This shift led to a conversation with a seasoned professional who later became a mentor and a valuable connection in my network. Our relationship was built on mutual respect and a genuine interest in each other's professional growth. This experience taught me that the most meaningful and lasting connections come from a place of authenticity and mutual support.

Cultivating a Network of Mutual Growth

As we explore the nuances of networking and building professional relationships, let's approach each interaction with an open heart and a genuine interest in the other person. Let's foster connections not just for immediate gains but for the potential of mutual growth and learning.

Let's remember that every person we meet holds a universe of experiences, knowledge, and possibilities. By cultivating these relationships with care, respect, and reciprocity, we weave a network that is not only professionally rewarding but also personally enriching.

In mastering the art of networking and relationship building, we don't just expand our professional circle; we open doors to new perspectives, collaborations, and opportunities. Let's use our skills to nurture relationships that are based on more than just professional needs, creating a network that thrives on shared success and collective advancement. Let's build not just connections, but a community of professionals who support and inspire each other towards greater heights.

Chapter 11: Personal Communication

11.1 With Friends and Family

In the warm tapestry of our personal lives, communication with friends and family forms the golden threads that connect us. It's in these relationships where our words and actions weave patterns of love, support, and understanding. Effective communication in this realm is not just about speaking and listening; it's about connecting heart to heart.

The Language of Love and Support

Communicating with friends and family involves speaking the language of love and support. It's about expressing care, being there in times of need, and celebrating in times of joy. This language transcends words; it's conveyed through our actions, our presence, and our attention.

Listening with the Heart

In our interactions with those closest to us, listening becomes more than an act of hearing. It's an act of feeling, of understanding the unspoken emotions and the stories behind the words. Heartfelt listening creates a space where loved ones feel truly heard and valued.

Open and Honest Communication

Honesty, tempered with kindness, is the cornerstone of communication with friends and family. It's about being open about our feelings, sharing our thoughts respectfully, and addressing issues before they become conflicts. Honesty builds trust, a vital component in these precious relationships.

A Personal Story of Heartfelt Connection

I remember a time when open and heartfelt communication transformed my relationship with a close family member. We had drifted apart over the years, caught up in our busy lives. A family gathering presented an opportunity for a real conversation, a chance to reconnect.

We sat down, and I opened up about how much I missed our closeness. I spoke not just with words but with the language of nostalgia, sincerity, and longing. To my surprise, they shared similar feelings. This honest and open exchange bridged the gap that time and distance had created. It reminded me of the power of transparent, heartfelt communication in nurturing and healing our most cherished relationships.

Nurturing Bonds Through Communication

As we explore the intricacies of personal communication with friends and family, let's cherish these interactions as opportunities to strengthen our bonds. Let's use our words and actions to express love, offer support, and build understanding.

In mastering the art of communication in our personal lives, we don't just maintain relationships; we enrich them, creating a network of support, love, and mutual respect. Let's embrace each conversation as a chance to deepen these bonds, turning every word and every listening moment into a gesture of love and connection.

11.2 In Intimate Relationships

In the delicate dance of intimate relationships, communication moves like a tender waltz, nuanced and profound. It's in these relationships that words carry not just meaning but the weight of emotions, desires and dreams. Effective communication in intimate relationships is about creating a harmony where love, understanding, and connection flourish

The Language of Vulnerability

In intimate relationships, communication is deeply rooted in vulnerability. It's about opening up your heart, sharing your fears, hopes, and dreams. This vulnerability is not a weakness but a strength that fosters deeper emotional connections.

Active Listening: Hearing Beyond Words

Active listening in intimate relationships goes beyond mere attention to words. It's about tuning into the subtleties of tone, emotion, and unspoken feelings. It's a listening that involves the heart, where empathy and understanding are as important as the words being spoken

Expressing Needs and Desires

Clear communication of needs and desires is crucial in intimate relationships. It's about being honest and direct about what you need and want, while also being open and receptive to your partner's needs. This exchange builds a foundation of mutual respect and understanding.

A Personal Journey of Emotional Communication

I recall a phase in my relationship where communication had become routine and superficial. Recognizing this, my partner and I committed to deepening our conversations. We set aside time to talk openly about our feelings, fears, and aspirations.

This practice transformed our relationship. It opened up new layers of understanding and connection. We learned to communicate not just with words, but with empathy, patience, and love. This journey of emotional communication brought us closer, turning challenges into opportunities for growth and strengthening the bond we shared.

Cultivating a Garden of Understanding

As we explore communication in intimate relationships, let's approach it as an art of balancing honesty with empathy, vulnerability with strength. Let's use our words to build bridges of understanding, to express love and appreciation, and to nurture the bond we share.

In mastering the art of communication in intimate relationships, we don't just coexist with our partners; we grow with them. We create a garden where trust, love, and understanding bloom in abundance. Let's cherish every conversation as an opportunity to deepen our connection, turning every word into a pledge of love and every moment of listening into an embrace of the heart.

Chapter 12: Public Speaking and Presentation

12.1 Preparing and Delivering Effective Speeches

In the grand theater of public speaking, every speech is a performance, an opportunity to captivate, inspire, and leave a lasting impact. Preparing and delivering effective speeches is an art form, where words become the paint, and the stage becomes the canvas. It's an act that transcends merely conveying information; it becomes a powerful tool for connection and change.

Crafting Your Message

The heart of an effective speech lies in its message. It's about having a clear, compelling point that resonates with your audience. Crafting your message involves careful consideration of your purpose, your audience's needs, and the key takeaways you want to leave them with. It's about weaving a narrative that is both informative and inspiring.

Mastering the Art of Preparation

Preparation is the foundation upon which great speeches are built. It involves researching your topic thoroughly, organizing your ideas coherently, and practicing your delivery. Preparation is not just about mastering the material; it's about becoming comfortable and confident in your ability to convey it.

The Power of Personalization

Personalizing your speech means infusing it with your unique style and personality. It's about sharing personal stories, experiences, and anecdotes that bring your message to life. This personal touch connects you to your audience, making your speech not just heard, but felt.

A Personal Triumph in Public Speaking

I recall a pivotal moment when I delivered a speech at a major conference. The topic was close to my heart, but the scale of the event was daunting. I spent weeks preparing, honing my message, and infusing it with personal stories that illustrated my points.

The night before, I practiced in front of a mirror, focusing not just on what I was saying, but how I was saying it. The next day, as I stood on stage, I took a deep breath and began. My words flowed, not just from my notes, but from my experiences, my passion, and my heart.

The response was overwhelming. Audience members approached me afterward, sharing how my speech had resonated with them. This experience was a powerful reminder of the impact of preparation, personalization, and passion in public speaking.

The Art of Speaking to Inspire

As we learn about the art of preparing and delivering effective speeches, let's embrace the opportunity to not just speak, but to inspire. Let's use our words to paint pictures, to stir emotions, and to provoke thought.

In mastering the art of public speaking, we become more than just speakers; we become storytellers, influencers, and catalysts for change. Let's approach each speech as an opportunity to leave a mark on our audience, to ignite a spark of inspiration, and to create a moment that resonates far beyond the stage.

Let's commit to crafting our speeches with diligence and delivering them with passion, transforming every stage into a platform for impact and every audience into a community of engaged listeners. In doing so, we don't just convey messages; we create experiences that enlighten, engage, and empower.

12.2 Engaging the Audience

In the world of public speaking, engaging the audience is the magic that transforms a speech from a monologue into a dialogue, a shared experience. It's about creating a bond with the audience, captivating their attention, and making them feel like an integral part of the journey. Engaging the audience turns a presentation into a conversation, a narrative that resonates and remains memorable.

The Power of Connection

Creating a connection with your audience is the first step in engagement. It involves understanding their interests, their challenges, and what they hope to gain from your speech. This connection is fostered by showing empathy, addressing their concerns, and aligning your message with their aspirations.

Interactive Techniques

Incorporating interactive techniques such as asking questions, inviting feedback, or using audience participation activities can significantly enhance engagement. These techniques transform passive listeners into active participants, making your speech more dynamic and memorable.

The Art of Storytelling

Storytelling is a powerful tool to engage audiences. A good story can transport listeners to different worlds, stir emotions, and deliver messages in a way that is both entertaining and enlightening. It's about weaving your points into narratives that captivate and connect with the audience on a personal level.

A Personal Experience of Audience Engagement

I remember delivering a keynote speech on a topic I was deeply passionate about. However, the real challenge was to translate this passion into engagement with a diverse audience. I started with a story that was personal yet universal, drawing them into a narrative that mirrored their own experiences.

Throughout the speech, I interacted with the audience, asking questions, and encouraging them to share their thoughts. This approach turned the speech into a two-way conversation, with the audience actively participating and contributing. Their responses not only enriched the session but also made it more relatable and impactful.

This experience taught me the immense power of audience engagement. It was not just about delivering content; it was about creating an experience, a shared space where both speaker and listener could learn, grow, and be inspired.

Crafting Engaging Experiences

As we look into the art of engaging the audience in public speaking and presentation, let's remember that our goal is to create an experience that resonates. Let's strive to understand our audience, to connect with them not just intellectually but emotionally, and to transform our speeches into interactive and memorable journeys.

Let's use storytelling, interactive techniques, and genuine empathy to create a bond with our audience. In doing so, we move beyond the boundaries of traditional speaking, turning each presentation into an opportunity for connection, inspiration, and shared learning.

In mastering the art of audience engagement, we don't just speak to an audience; we speak with them, creating a symphony of shared experiences and mutual inspiration. Let's embrace each speaking opportunity as a chance to touch hearts, open minds, and leave a lasting impact.

V

Part V: Real-World Applications and Case Studies

Chapter 13: Case Studies of Effective Communication

13.1 Analysis of Real-Life Scenarios

In the vibrant landscape of human interaction, real-life scenarios of effective communication shine as beacons, guiding and inspiring us. Analyzing these scenarios is like unraveling a tapestry, revealing the intricate patterns and techniques that make communication truly effective. Each scenario is a lesson, a story of triumph and transformation through the power of words and understanding.

The Symphony of Corporate Crisis Management

One remarkable case study revolves around a corporate crisis. A major company faced a public relations nightmare due to a product malfunction. The potential for brand damage was immense. However, the company's response turned the situation around. Their communication was swift, transparent, and empathetic. They acknowledged the issue, communicated their plan to address it, and expressed genuine concern for those affected. This approach not only mitigated the crisis but also strengthened the trust of customers and stakeholders.

This scenario underscores the power of transparency and empathy in crisis communication. It shows how taking responsibility and offering clear, compassionate responses can transform a potential disaster into an opportunity for building trust and credibility.

The Dance of Diplomatic Negotiation

Another insightful case involves diplomatic negotiations between two countries with a history of tension. The diplomats used a strategy of respectful listening, acknowledging each other's perspectives, and focusing on common goals rather than differences. Their communication was characterized by diplomatic language, cultural sensitivity, and patience.

This case teaches us the importance of respect and empathy in communication, especially in sensitive situations. It highlights how understanding and acknowledging different perspectives can lead to breakthroughs in even the most challenging negotiations.

The Harmony of Healthcare Communication

A healthcare scenario provides a powerful lesson in empathetic communication. A doctor, dealing with a patient's complex and emotional health issue, employed a communication style that was both informative and incredibly empathetic. The doctor listened intently, explained the medical situation clearly, and addressed the patient's fears and concerns with genuine compassion.

This case illustrates the impact of empathy and clarity in healthcare communication. It shows how healthcare professionals can provide comfort and understanding alongside crucial medical information enhancing patient care and trust.

The Art of Learning from Real-Life Communication

As we learn about these and other real-life case studies, let's draw inspiration and lessons from each. Let's understand that effective communication is a blend of clarity, empathy, respect, and understanding.

In analyzing these scenarios, we not only learn the strategies and techniques that make communication effective but also appreciate the profound impact that our words and actions can have on individuals, communities, and even nations.

Let's use these lessons to refine our communication skills, aiming not just to convey messages, but to connect, inspire, and transform. Each real-life scenario is a story of communication's power to overcome challenges, bridge divides, and create positive change. Let's embrace these stories as guides on our path to becoming more effective and empathetic communicators.

13.2 Lessons Learned from Each Case

In the vast landscape of communication, each case study is like a lighthouse, illuminating the path to effective interaction. The lessons learned from these real-life scenarios are not just strategies or techniques; they are guiding principles that can transform the way we interact, connect, and understand each other in every facet of life.

The Resilience of Transparency and Empathy

From the corporate crisis scenario, the paramount lesson is the resilience fostered by transparency and empathy. It teaches us that in times of crisis, being open, honest, and empathetic not only helps in managing the situation but also builds long-term trust and credibility.

The Power of Respectful Listening and Common Ground

The diplomatic negotiation case highlights the significance of respectful listening and finding common ground. This scenario serves as a reminder that even in the face of conflict, taking the time to understand different perspectives and focusing on shared goals can lead to peaceful and mutually beneficial outcomes.

Empathy and Clarity in Sensitive Situations

The healthcare communication case illustrates the crucial role of empathy and clarity, especially in sensitive situations. It underscores the importance of addressing concerns with compassion and providing clear, understandable information, which can significantly improve the experience and outcome for those involved.

The Transformative Effect of Effective Communication

Each of these case studies reinforces that effective communication is transformative. Whether it's in crisis management, diplomatic negotiations, or healthcare, the way we communicate can change outcomes, perceptions, and relationships.

A Personal Reflection on Communication's Impact

Reflecting on these lessons, I recall a personal experience where clear, empathetic communication made a significant difference. I was part of a team handling a complex project with multiple stakeholders. Differences in opinion and miscommunication had led to a tense atmosphere. By applying these lessons - focusing on transparent communication, actively listening to each team member, and empathizing with their concerns - we were able to turn the situation around. The project was not only completed successfully but also strengthened our team's dynamics.

Embracing the Lessons in Our Communication Journey

As we embrace the lessons from these case studies, let's approach our communication with the intention to be clear, empathetic, respectful, and understanding. Let's remember that each word we speak, each message we convey, holds the power to impact, influence, and inspire.

In integrating these lessons into our daily communication, we not only enhance our interactions but also contribute to a more understanding and connected world. Let's use these insights to elevate our communication, transforming every conversation into an opportunity for positive change and deeper connection.

Chapter 14: Developing Your Communication Plan

14.1 Personal Assessment and Goal Setting

In the pursuit of mastering the art of communication, the first step is akin to setting sail on a vast ocean of potential. It begins with personal assessment and goal setting – a process of introspection, understanding where you are, and envisioning where you want to be. This stage is not just about setting targets; it's about igniting a passion for personal growth and transformation.

The Mirror of Self-Assessment

Self-assessment in communication is like holding up a mirror to your skills, habits, and patterns. It involves asking yourself honest questions about your strengths and areas for improvement. Are you an active listener? How effectively do you express your thoughts and emotions? This reflective process is the foundation upon which you can build a robust communication plan.

Charting Your Goals

Goal setting in communication is about creating specific, measurable, achievable, relevant, and time-bound (SMART) objectives. It's about defining what success looks like for you. Whether it's becoming more articulate, improving your listening skills, or mastering the art of persuasion, your goals should be clear and motivating.

A Personal Story of Transformation

I remember a time when my public speaking skills were a significant barrier in my career. Recognizing this, I embarked on a journey of self-improvement. I began with a frank assessment of my fears and shortcomings and set a goal to speak at a major conference within a year.

This goal propelled me into action – I attended workshops, sought feedback, and practiced relentlessly. The process was challenging, but my commitment to my goal kept me anchored. When the day of the conference arrived, and I stepped onto the stage, it was not just a speech I was delivering; it was a testament to the power of personal assessment and goal setting.

Embarking on Your Communication Odyssey

As we navigate through the process of personal assessment and goal setting, let's approach it with an open mind and a willingness to grow. Let's set goals that challenge and excite us, that push us to uncover the full potential of our communicative abilities.

In undertaking this journey of self-improvement, remember that every step, every bit of progress, is a leap towards becoming the communicator you aspire to be. Let's embrace this process not just as a task, but as an opportunity to unlock new horizons in our personal and professional lives. Let each goal be a milestone in our quest to master the art of communication, a skill that can open doors, bridge gaps, and create lasting impacts.

14.2 Continuous Improvement and Practice

In the evolving journey of communication, continuous improvement and practice stand as the pillars of progress and excellence. This commitment to growth is not just about refining skills; it's about nurturing a lifelong passion for learning and self-development. It's a path that leads not only to better communication but to a richer, more fulfilling life experience.

The Cycle of Continuous Improvement

Continuous improvement in communication is a cyclical process of learning, applying, getting feedback, and refining. It's about embracing the mindset of a perpetual student, always curious, always open to learning. This process involves seeking out new knowledge, techniques and insights that can enhance your communication skills.

The Power of Practice

Practice is the crucible in which great communicators are forged. I involves putting what you've learned into action, whether it's through speaking engagements, writing, or everyday conversations. Regular practice helps in internalizing new skills, making them a natural part of your communication repertoire.

Creating Opportunities for Growth

Seek out opportunities for practicing and improving your communication skills. This could be in professional settings like meetings and presentations, or personal scenarios like social gatherings or volunteer work. Each situation is a chance to apply, test, and refine your skills.

A Personal Story of Growth Through Practice

I recall a period when I sought to improve my ability to persuade and inspire audiences. I joined a local speaking club, where I could practice regularly in a supportive environment. Each speech was an opportunity to experiment with new techniques, receive constructive feedback, and see my progress over time.

This commitment to regular practice transformed my speaking abilities. I became more confident, articulate, and impactful. But more than that, it transformed my approach to learning and personal development, turning it into a fulfilling and continuous journey.

Embracing the Path of Lifelong Learning

As we embrace the process of continuous improvement and practice, let's view it as an exhilarating adventure in self-discovery and personal mastery. Let's recognize that each step forward in improving our communication skills is a step toward realizing our full potential.

In committing to this path of lifelong learning, we not only become more effective communicators; we become more engaged, more empathetic, and more connected individuals. Let's cherish each opportunity to practice and improve as a gift, a chance to hone our craft and contribute more meaningfully to the world around us. Let every word we speak and every interaction we have be a reflection of our commitment to continuous growth and excellence in communication.

Conclusion - The Path Forward in Effective Communication

Summarizing Key Takeaways

As we draw the curtains on this exploration of effective communication, let us pause and reflect on the key takeaways that form the essence of this journey. These are not mere points of learning; they are beacons to guide us in the art of connecting, understanding, and influencing.

The Symphony of Communication Skills

The first takeaway is the multifaceted nature of communication. We've seen how verbal and non-verbal elements, listening skills, empathy, persuasion, and emotional intelligence all play harmonious roles in effective communication. Like instruments in an orchestra, each contributes to the melody of successful interactions.

The Dance of Continuous Improvement

Another crucial takeaway is the importance of continuous improvement and practice. Communication skills are akin to a garden that requires regular tending. With consistent practice, feedback, and a willingness to learn, our ability to communicate can grow and flourish.

The Power of Authenticity and Empathy

We have also discovered the transformative power of authenticity and empathy in communication. By being genuine in our interactions and striving to understand others, we build bridges of trust and create deeper, more meaningful connections.

A Personal Reflection on Communication's Impact

Reflecting on my journey, I recall a personal experience that encapsulates these takeaways. I was tasked with mediating a challenging situation in my community. Employing active listening, empathy, and clear, honest communication, I was able to facilitate a dialogue that transformed conflict into understanding. This experience reinforced my belief in the power of effective communication to create positive change.

Embracing the Future of Communication

As we move forward, let us carry these takeaways as tools and inspirations. Let's approach every conversation, every speech, and every written word as an opportunity to practice and refine our skills.

Let's commit to being lifelong learners in the art of communication, understanding that each interaction is an opportunity to connect more deeply, understand more profoundly, and influence more positively.

In embracing the path forward in effective communication, we open ourselves to a world of possibilities. A world where our words and actions can build, heal, inspire, and transform. Let's step into this world with confidence, with the knowledge and skills we've gained, and with the excitement of all that we have yet to learn and achieve.

Encouragement for Ongoing Development

As we stand at the threshold of concluding this enlightening exploration of effective communication, let us look forward with a spirit of optimism and a commitment to continuous growth. The path of enhancing our communication skills is an ongoing journey, one filled with endless opportunities for learning, connecting, and transforming not just our interactions, but our lives.

The Canvas of Lifelong Learning

Remember, the art of communication is like a vast canvas, ever-expanding and evolving. Each day presents new scenarios, challenges, and opportunities to apply and refine our skills. Embrace these moments, for they are the crucibles in which exceptional communicators are forged.

The Tapestry of Diverse Experiences

Life, in its beautiful complexity, offers a tapestry of diverse experiences, each enriching our understanding and ability to communicate. Engage with different cultures, perspectives, and environments. These experiences deepen our empathy, broaden our understanding, and enhance our ability to connect with a wide range of individuals.

A Personal Narrative of Continuous Growth

I recall a period in my life where I consciously decided to challenge my communication abilities. I sought opportunities to speak to varied audiences, engaged in conversations on complex topics, and listened to stories vastly different from my own. This commitment to continuous learning and exposure to diverse situations significantly sharpened my communication skills and broadened my worldview.

The Beacon of Self-Reflection and Adaptability

As you move forward, let self-reflection be your guiding beacon. Regularly assess your communication style, adapt to various situations, and be open to feedback. This adaptability is crucial in an ever-changing world, allowing you to communicate effectively in any circumstance.

The Journey Towards Communicative Excellence

Finally, let us stride forward with confidence and determination on this endless journey towards communicative excellence. Believe in your potential to grow, to influence positively, and to connect deeply. The skills you cultivate today will be the tools that help you build a better tomorrow, not just for yourself but for the communities and networks you are a part of.

In embracing ongoing development in communication, we embrace a future brimming with possibilities. A future where our words and actions resonate with clarity, empathy, and understanding. Let's step into this future with the knowledge that our journey of growth and learning is one of the most profound investments we can make in ourselves and our shared world.

What Are Your Thoughts?

I invite you to take a moment to reflect. Has this journey through the art of communication enlightened you or inspired a change in how you connect with the world? If these pages have enriched your understanding, I'd be grateful for your shared experience in an Amazon review. Your insights are truly invaluable. Thank you for your time and consideration; your feedback is cherished.

With Warm Regards,

Saif Hussaini

Made in the USA
Las Vegas, NV
09 April 2024